BREAKING THE SILENCE

BOOKS BY CECIL MURPHEY

Breaking the Silence:
Spiritual Help When Someone You Love
Is Mentally Ill

Keeping My Balance:
Spiritual Help When Someone I Love
Abuses Drugs

Day to Day
Spiritual Help When Someone You Love
Has Alzheimer's

Another Chance:
Learning to Like Yourself

BREAKING
THE SILENCE

*SPIRITUAL HELP
WHEN SOMEONE YOU LOVE
IS MENTALLY ILL*

CECIL MURPHEY

Westminster/John Knox Press
Louisville, Kentucky

The scripture quotation marked NIV is from the *Holy Bible, New International Version.* Copyright © 1973, 1978, International Bible Society.

The scripture quotation marked TEV is from *Good News Bible: The Bible in Today's English Version.* Old Testament: © American Bible Society, 1976; New Testament: © American Bible Society, 1966, 1971, 1976.

Book design by Gene Harris

First edition

Published by Westminster/John Knox Press
Louisville, Kentucky

PRINTED IN THE UNITED STATES OF AMERICA

9 8 7 6 5 4 3 2 1

Library of Congress Cataloging-in-Publication Data

Murphey, Cecil B.
  Breaking the silence.

  Bibliography: p.
  1. Mentally ill—Family relationships—Prayer-books and devotions—English. I. Title.
BV4908.5.M85 1989 242'.86 88-17294
ISBN 0-664-21329-4 (hard)

CONTENTS

ONE

FIRST FOCUS

SICK DENIALS

He was only fourteen the first time he said, "I think I'm crazy or something."

"Everybody feels like that at times," I said.

For the next three years my son tried to tell me in different ways that he was mentally ill, but I refused to hear and, instead, resorted to quick words of reassurance. "You'll grow out of this."

I played the game of denial. I couldn't believe that *my* wonderful child needed psychiatric treatment.

When the school counselor said, "He has serious problems and needs help," I finally stopped my denial.

God, forgive me for ignoring the truth. Help me to listen to his cries of pain no matter how much I don't want to hear. Amen.

YOU DON'T NEED TO BE HERE

The doctor explained my wife's diagnosis and told me the name of the medicine they were giving her. When I asked about getting her out of the hospital, he said, "We'll have to talk about that later."

"But she's not sick, really sick," I said.

"She's very sick," he said emphatically.

When I saw my wife, I said, "I know you've been under a strain and you're high-strung, but you don't need to be here—not like all these sick people."

"I do need to be here," she said. "I'm as sick as any of the others."

After several long talks with her doctor, I stopped denying that she was deeply depressed and that she was getting worse.

Now, four months later, I'm glad the doctor insisted. She is better. They were both right: she needed to be there.

God, help me to accept her needs and not try to deny her illness. Amen.

UNHEARD CRIES

I went through a night of torment. When I arrived home earlier than expected, I found his suicide note that read, "I can't take it any more." I called the paramedics, and they rushed him to the hospital in time. I sat all night in the room with him and asked myself questions.

Why? Did I fail him? These things don't just happen. My son must have been troubled a long time and I didn't know—or didn't want to know.

Looking backward, I recalled examples of bizarre behavior. He had been trying to tell me for a long time—through cries I didn't hear, such as his odd behavior and confused conversation. I turned deaf until he broke through the silence in the only way he knew how.

God, thank you that he is alive so that I can now listen. With your help, I won't seal him into silence again. Amen.

TOO YOUNG

I didn't know how to talk to the doctor about her. I could only describe her bizarre symptoms. Days later the doctor said, "Your daughter is mentally ill. She is schizophrenic."

The words ripped me apart and I cried out, "But she's too young. She's only twenty-one!"

"Do you think mental illness is a disease of the elderly?" the doctor asked in his calm voice. "Schizophrenia shows up anywhere, from the teens to the twenties in males and for females in the mid to late twenties."

He described her as having *process* schizophrenia, meaning she showed signs of trouble early in life. Now the classic features of delusions and uncontrolled excitement have emerged. Within minutes she reverts from speaking in a flat voice to euphoria.

God, she is so young. Give us whatever we need to support her lovingly in all the stages of her life. Amen.

ADMITTING IT

They called me strong. Brave. Kind. I loved hearing words like that. I put up with a husband who underwent psychiatric treatment in the hospital five times. I never complained. Everyone said I smiled in the face of adversity.

But I was presenting a beautiful facade, although I didn't realize it then. I persistently pushed away my own pain and gave the world a bright smile.

Last week, his therapist talked to me and refused to allow me to lie to myself any longer. "You're hurting," he said. "He has embarrassed and angered you. Don't hold back; it's all right to admit it."

"Yes," I said through my tears. I had pushed the pain away and hidden the hurt from myself. Now I am getting help in facing my true feelings.

God, I want to be caring and supportive. I need your grace in my neediness so that I can help him with his problems. Amen.

WHO'S SICK?

I didn't know what her therapist would tell me to do, but I never expected what he did say: "Get help for yourself."

"Me?" I replied in shock. "I'm not the sick one. I haven't gone through terrible depressions and—"

"No," he said softly, "you're not sick. But you need help too." When I continued to balk he said, "Look at it this way. The more help you get, the more you can cope with her. Furthermore, mental illness—or any kind of illness—affects everyone in the family. If she had suffered a massive coronary and I suggested you attend a seminar, you wouldn't hesitate. So get help—immediately."

I did as he suggested. Besides seeing a therapist, I am also getting help from a support group of families of mentally ill patients. I've learned a lot about her problem.

God, I'm glad I got help because I'm stronger now. Show me how to use my newfound strength in helping her. Amen.

PULL YOURSELF OUT

I must have said to him fifty times, "If you'd make up your mind that you're okay, you could snap out of it."

One day his eyes filled with tears and he said, "Do you think I like being this way? That I choose to be sick and a burden? If I had a broken leg, you wouldn't demand that I make up my mind to be well and then start walking."

The shock from those words made me face how cruelly I had spoken. He was sick and didn't have the choice of pulling himself together. I had been wrong; I apologized, and I've never said those words again.

Once I stopped demanding that he pull himself out of his mental problems, we began to work together. He is going to get better, and I'm with him all the way.

Wise God, thank you that the patient had the courage to tell the caregiver what she needed to hear. Give us both guidance as we struggle in this together. Amen.

CAREFUL WORDS

I determined never to use words like *crazy* or *insane* around her. Mom had been through a lot in the past two years. I said "when you were away" or "your illness."

The rest of the family picked up my cue, and we chose our words so that we wouldn't remind her of her painful ordeal.

Once I laughingly said to my brother, "Oh, you're crazy." As soon as the words passed my lips I felt terrible.

"Compared to me, he's fine," Mom said. "Back there I was so crazy I fought getting a shot because I thought you were paying them to kill me. Another patient laughed and said, 'That's insane. Who would spend that much money to get rid of you?'"

Mom's freedom to say *crazy* and *insane* set us free from choosing our words so carefully.

God, we love Mom. Thank you that she has taught us that we can be ourselves around her—just the way we are around you. Amen.

EUPHEMISMS

We couldn't face the shame of mental illness in our family, so we became experts at avoiding having to speak about it. We used words like *indisposed* or *convalescent.*

If he's not normal, we secretly wondered, then what about the rest of us? What about our children? So we opted for nice words to disguise the horror of his situation.

When he came home for a weekend I referred to his *resting* and his *trip.* On the second day he screamed at me, "I'm sick! Sick! Sick! I'm a mental patient in a psychiatric hospital!"

He forced me to face the reality of his condition. Our using euphemisms—nice, cover-up words—had enabled us to continue to deny the truth of his illness.

God, thank you for helping me to see that in some ways he's healthier than I am. He is mentally ill, and I need to recognize and call it by name as I continue to care for him. Amen.

STIGMA

My sister is not violent; she *is* schizophrenic. She talks to herself in public, convinced that evil forces plot against her and that everyone hears what she says.

It's enough of a burden to have a mentally ill family member. Some look upon us as the cause of her illness. Either my parents passed on bad genes (as if they had a choice) or they mistreated her. I'm tired of people asking if anyone sexually or physically abused my sister. I'm tired of being asked, "Is she the only one?" as if they expected me to say, "Oh, no, every fourth person born in our family is mentally off balance."

We didn't do everything right in our home, but she received the same kind of treatment we all had and we're normal. She's sick and we have to bear the stigma. And it hurts.

God, forgive me for complaining, but today is one of those days when I hurt too much to face the insensitivity of others. Hold me close, God, until I get past this. Amen.

HOW LONG?

The doctor explained everything thoroughly, but I kept waiting for one answer. Finally I asked, "How long will he need treatment?"

"I have no way of knowing," she said. "Some people need medication their entire lives; others require drugs only periodically. I can't promise you an end to treatment. Our goal is to help the mentally ill achieve the highest degree of independence and productivity possible."

The words saddened me, although I knew she spoke honestly. I didn't get the answer I wanted, but I know that the medical profession, along with our network of friends, is with us in our day-to-day struggles.

God, I still cry out, "How long?" I want him well and, even though I don't see an immediate cure, hope still springs up, assuring me that one day he will get better. Amen.

CURE?

Will she be cured? Ever? I think about this often. Her doctor avoids answering and says things like "She's improving" or "She'll adjust." Doesn't he hear my real question?

I want my wife *cured*. I don't want the threat of another attack hanging over our lives. If someone—anyone—would just say to me, "She is going to be cured," I could be at rest. But no one will say that. I suppose no one can guarantee the results. But is there no cure for mental illness? Do they only adjust, cope, and improve? We get physically sick and we recover. Why can't I know the same thing about mental illness?

Finally I asked myself, "If I knew the answer, would it make a difference?" Whether she was sick or cured, I'd still treat her lovingly. That's when I stopped asking the question.

God, I've demanded ultimate answers, and you keep trying to teach me to live in the immediate moment. Be patient with me; I'm learning. Amen.

FOR WHOSE GOOD?

I didn't tell our relatives about our son's mental problems. They all live out of state, and when they phoned I made excuses for his not being there. I think I covered it well. I'm doing this for our son's good, I told myself.

I told his doctor what I had done, and she assured me that many families go through this cover-up. "There are better ways of handling this," she said. She helped me to find a support group where I could talk about my needs. *And about him.*

One day I faced a hard fact. I hadn't withheld the truth for his good or for the relatives' protection. I did it because of my inability to admit how sick he was. Now the whole family knows. To my surprise, they have offered *me* as much support and comfort as they have him!

God, I was afraid for him but just as much for myself. I still get afraid at times. Give me the strength and the courage I need to face each day. Amen.

WHO AM I?

I used to define myself as a father, a husband, or a male. Since my daughter's illness I am also the doctor, the nurse, the social worker, the friend, and the jailer. I am so many people wrapped into one that I no longer ask, Who *am* I?

At the hospital they diagnosed my daughter as suffering from major affective disorder. The word *affective* refers to her moods, which change from extreme sadness (depression) to excitement and increased activity (mania). She's sick, and I'm doing everything I can to help. But caring for her places so many demands upon me I constantly feel exhausted.

I want to shut the door of my bedroom and wish I never had to face her and her problems again. Yet I can't do that. I have a daughter whom I love, and I can't forsake her when she needs me.

God, I'm as confused in my own way as my daughter is in hers. Help her as you give me strength to do what I can. Amen.

SECONDHAND FAITH

I wanted to believe he would get better, perhaps have a total recovery, but I could not conjure up such assurance.

I talked with my husband's therapist (who attends our church) and told her how I felt. "I believe he will get better," she said.

"Can you guarantee it?" I asked.

"No," she said. "But I have faith."

I knew that I did not have faith—not that kind anyway. The therapist was so peaceful and confident. She truly believed.

"Okay," I said, "I don't have faith myself but I have faith in your faith. If you're able to believe in his getting better, I'm going to believe in your belief in him."

God, I know that's secondhand faith, but it's the best I can do now. At least secondhand faith is faith, isn't it? Amen.

ASHAMED

"You never talk about your wife," a co-worker said. "You mention your children, your hobbies, but not your wife. Don't you get along?"

"We get along fine," I said and changed the subject. I was too ashamed to tell him that my wife is mentally ill. I didn't talk about her condition with anyone. I told our church friends she had gone to visit relatives "for a month or so."

Somehow our pastor found out she was in a psychiatric hospital, and he visited me. He said to me later, "It must be a heavy load that you're carrying—all by yourself. I wish you'd let us share your pain."

"I'm too ashamed," I said—the first time I had admitted that to myself. "Ashamed of what people will think. Of her. Of me. Ashamed of feeling this way."

"I can tell you only that *I* know about your wife, and I love you both," he told me.

God, thank you for someone who cares. His caring has helped me open up to others. Amen.

MRS. NEVER-WRONG

"You're so absolutely perfect," said my sick son. "You have all the answers even when I don't have questions. You never make mistakes like the rest of us mortals. You're Mrs. Never-Wrong!"

His tirade went on and on, but I didn't hear anything after that. I'd known for a long time how important it is for me to be right. Some of that came from my own childhood, where I felt I was never right. Yet it went deeper with me. I had trouble admitting mistakes. I didn't easily say, "I'm wrong and I'm sorry."

I've argued for hours with people, "proving" I was right. Now I'm becoming aware that to admit I'm wrong holds terror for me. I believed that to say I was wrong meant I had failed. I now know that if I fail in one incident, I haven't failed in everything. I finally learned to say, "I was wrong."

God of all knowledge, keep teaching me that I don't have to know everything. Help me see that only you are right one hundred percent of the time. Amen.

SOMETHING WRONG

I kept thinking, I've done something wrong. I must have caused her problems. If not caused them, added to them. I analyzed everything I did—or didn't do—and treated myself rather harshly.

"It's not your fault," she said. "It's my problem, my weakness."

Her doctor counseled, "You didn't do anything wrong—not in the sense of causing any of her problems. Besides, we're not looking for someone to blame. I'm expecting your support in helping her get better."

I've since been combating my constant guilt —the sense of having done something wrong. I grew up in a family where I felt responsible for everything that went wrong, regardless of whether I could do anything about it.

Our wise doctor wrote me a prescription: Say the following three times before every meal: *I am doing the best I can, and my best is enough.*

God, thanks for this prescription. Make it effective. Amen.

IF ONLY I HAD BEEN PERFECT

When did I pick up the idea that I had to be perfect? Perhaps because as a child I could never do anything good enough so I tried harder.

When he became ill, I blamed myself for his problems. One day after I had complained to my support group about how badly I had failed, the leader asked, "Do you realize how often you have made *if* statements?" He pointed out three of them, and I had a lot more that I used on myself:

- If I had been a better wife
- If I had been more sensitive to him
- If I had gotten help sooner
- If I had been more helpful
- If I had been more patient

The leader smiled. "If you had been perfect you wouldn't have to make *if* statements."

The group helped me to understand that most conscientious people have similar feelings.

God, thank you for sending these friends who showed me how to admit my imperfections. Help me to accept myself as I am—just the way you have always accepted me. Amen.

COP-OUT

I've been struggling with my anger toward her for a long time. When things get tough I have to fight. She cops out by checking into the mental ward. And that makes me really mad.

Why can't she carry her load? She lies in a hospital bed or walks around like a zombie while I hold down a job, try to take care of three children, and still visit her. Then I feel guilty for feeling this way. She didn't do this on purpose, and she didn't do it to make me mad.

I talked to our pastor, and she said, "I would feel the same way. It's normal to be angry at such behavior. Admitting your anger is the first step toward resolving the issue."

I still get frustrated with the load; I want her healthy. I wish life weren't working this way. But I am learning to accept her way of trying to cope.

God of all emotions, help me admit my feelings, no matter how negative they are. Make me healthy so I can help her on the way to health. Amen.

MOTHER LOAD

I sensed our son's behavior was not quite normal. My husband insisted, "He only needs a little more discipline."

As our son grew worse, my husband emotionally separated himself, refusing to see the obvious. His work schedule increased; he left early in the morning and returned after dark. He had little to say. Any initiative on my part met with, "I had a hard day. Let me rest."

More than once I cried myself to sleep because I believed that mates were meant to share each other's burdens.

Through a self-help group, I discovered that most of the women there knew the tyranny of the "mother load."

My husband remains aloof. Our son is undergoing psychiatric and drug treatment, so I still carry the mother load.

God, I can bear this load with your help and through the supportive love of my friends. Yet I still wish you'd help my husband to become part of the solution too. Amen.

SHE DID THIS TO US

She's sick and has been undergoing treatment for five years. As her husband, I've tried to be supportive and sensitive. Only recently, however, I finally admitted an emotion trapped deep inside: I was angry—at her.

This awareness came in my therapy group when the leader reacted to me by saying, "It sounds like you're angry."

I denied it but she kept probing, and finally I screamed, "I *am* angry! She did this to us. She ruined my life!"

I didn't want to feel that way and before I could apologize, the therapist said, "Most family caregivers go through that. Your wife has disrupted your life. You can talk about your feelings here and let us help you to cope."

God, thank you for my support group, because they are just that—a support. Without you and them, I couldn't face her illness. Amen.

IF ONLY I HAD . . .

"We all react differently to pressure," the caseworker assured me. "He turned the pressure inward, and that led to his mental illness."

More than once I heard the comforting words that tried to assure me I had done nothing wrong. Yet I thought, If only I had noticed his behavior earlier. If only I had insisted he see a doctor. If only I had been kinder and more sensitive. Logic told me that my earlier awareness would not have made much overall difference and that going over the what-if facts now wouldn't help. Yet my emotions still churned.

The caseworker suggested I reverse the what-if approach by asking what if I had forever ignored his problem? What if I had refused to get help for him? What if I hadn't cared? Those answers have helped to make his situation easier for me to accept.

God, deliver me from my torturous questions and remind me that I did the best I knew how. With your help, I'm going to be more sensitive to his needs. Amen.

ERASING MISTAKES

If I counted up the mistakes I've made with our daughter, what would be the total? Quite a few—perhaps in the thousands. For the first year after her diagnosis and treatment, I made many errors by saying the wrong things. I pushed too hard and demanded too much. I wish I could go back and erase all the wrongs.

A friend in my support group said, "You haven't caused irrevocable damage. You only made mistakes. The two are different. You can now learn to be more lovingly supportive and actually erase the mistakes."

My friend understood exactly what I was going through. The new level of loving communication with my daughter tells me that she has wiped away my errors too.

Forgiving God, you set the standard by forgiving us. Now help me to wipe away the errors of my past. Amen.

PITY PARTY

I laughed when Rita told our support group about her pity party. When the pressures build up so that she's at the end of it all, she turns off the phone and goes into her den. She holds up a mirror and talks to it. "Nobody knows the strain I'm under and nobody cares." Until she runs out of reasons, she tells her image how terrible her life has been and still is and how she has a right to feel depressed because of overwork and under-appreciation.

When she runs out of self-pitying thoughts, she makes faces in the mirror and ends up laughing at herself.

Rita's way is not mine, but she has found a method to cope with times of self-pity. We all have those terrible times, and Rita has given me hope to know that I can win over my moments of self-pity.

Caring God, it's easy for me to feel sorry for myself—and I do at times. Teach me to do it in a healthy way so that I can be more faithful to you and supportive of my husband. Amen.

DEMANDING LOVE

"God, if she would get even a little better, I'd be encouraged." She got worse. I became more demanding in my prayers and, I suspect, more demanding of her. She got still worse.

One day when she was lucid, she said, "You don't love me and I'm sorry I have to put you through this. I wish I'd die; it would be easier for everybody."

I hurriedly assured her that I loved her and didn't want her to die. Afterward I probed my heart. *Did* I love her? Yes, I answered, I do.

Why couldn't she believe I love her? I knew why: my kind of love made demands. I offered a love with conditions tied to it: Get better and you'll get more love.

I'm slowly changing. I began by saying, "I love you. I'll always be here for you, no matter how you behave."

Did she improve after that? Or did my change make it seem that way? She is better now— and so am I.

God, because you accepted me, I'm learning to accept her exactly as she is now. *Amen.*

DEATH WISH

After months of deep inner turmoil, I finally said the words aloud in prayer: "I wish he'd die!"

For a few minutes my imagination soared with the thoughts of the freedom and peace I would enjoy.

Then my feelings vacillated between guilt and desire. I had put up with him for so long I was worn out. He had alienated our children. He had no friends left. I don't *really* want him to die. But once in a while, when the pressure gets heavy and he has an especially bad day, I think about his death.

In my support group, others told me they had similar fantasies. Knowing that I'm not the only one who has such moments helps me in my struggle with guilt feelings.

Omniscient God, you know my thoughts better than I do. Thank you for helping me accept my need to feel as I do. Amen.

FORGIVING

I ought to forgive her. God tells me to; my friends and family say I must. She's begged me to forgive. "I want to," I said, "but I can't let go. You put me through too much pain just to forget it and go on as if it never happened."

I promised her I would try—and I did, but resentment and anger built up again. Today I figured out something. I have not truly wanted to forgive. I liked being angry and forcing her to try to please me. I'm ashamed of myself, but now that I understand myself better, I can let go. I don't have to hold on any more.

God, you are always ready to forgive. I'm sorry it's taken me so long to want to wipe away all her mistakes. Help me to put away all the past hurts. Amen.

RESPONSIBLE LIMITS

I wonder how often I grumbled about his not taking responsibility. I picked up and laundered his clothes, cleaned his room, cooked his meals. I grumbled about him whenever anyone asked how he was doing. I constantly felt exhausted doing everything for him.

Then a friend said, "People will only be as responsible as we let them."

"But if I didn't do all these things for him, they would never get done!"

"So what?" my friend said.

She helped me to face a harsh reality. I had limited his responsibility because he was not reliable. But then, he didn't have to be. The more I did for him, the more I hindered his progress.

Then I told him, "From now on, you are going to do things for yourself." He still doesn't take full responsibility, but he is getting better.

God, he is responsible to himself and to you. Don't let me forget that—ever. Amen.

THE 49-PERCENT RULE

I'm the helper type, willing to do anything I can. Sometimes I do too much despite our doctor's warning, "Don't do too much for her."

Unfortunately, I found myself taking on more work, trying to make her life a little easier. For instance, on her worst days, I let her lie in bed and waited on her. Now I realize that, had she gotten out of bed and done things for herself, she would have benefited.

Our doctor finally said, "Don't do more than 49 percent of any task. You can help, but she must learn to do things herself." Few things have caused me more trouble than holding to the 49-percent rule. I kept wanting to do just a little more. But I did insist she do things for herself. "If you have trouble, I'm here."

She's now much better. She's working part-time—a job she found by herself. I drive her to the bus line, and she goes the rest of the way alone.

Loving God, help me hold to the 49-percent rule—no matter how hard. Amen.

ENOUGH?

Am I doing enough? How much is enough? When do I cross the line and do too much? I don't know the answers to those questions— which is why I still have problems in coping when he sinks into one of his deep, depressed moods.

I try to build up his confidence and then wonder later if I've undermined him by doing too much. Or hurt him by not doing quite enough. And who can tell where to draw the line? I can't ask him. My friends aren't any surer than I am.

I have decided that, no matter what comes up, I don't do *everything* for him. If I insist that he put forth some effort, at least I know I'm closer to doing "enough." Instead of enjoying peace of mind, I often worry that I'm not doing what's most beneficial for him.

God of all peace, I don't want to fail him by doing too much or too little. Give me your peace and guidance so that I'll do just enough. Amen.

EXPECTATIONS

"She's not getting any better," I said. After two years I resigned myself to the way things were.

When friends asked, "How's she doing?" my best answer was, "About the same." To the question about progress, I shook my head. Six months ago a friend said, "As long as you're satisfied that she won't improve, she probably won't."

What a burden he had laid on me—as if I determined her condition! And yet, I finally admitted, I did have something to do with progress.

Others who have mentally ill family members agreed with my friend. "You set the tone," one person said. "If you expect her to get better and help her, she does improve."

Since then I have been seeing slight signs of improvement. How much of it has come about because of my expectations?

God, I don't understand how my expectations affect her health, but they do. Help me to expect the best for her, always. Amen.

VACATION?

While I waited for the druggist to fill a prescription, two women, also waiting, talked about their upcoming vacations. One family planned to go to Mexico and the other to Europe.

I'd be excited just to have a day off, I thought. One whole day when I didn't have to think about my husband's problems. One day to do only as I pleased. But I don't have vacations. I work 168 hours a week caring for him.

Some days he does so well that I hardly notice the strain. But the roller coaster starts again after a week or a month. So I take mini-vacations by spending an afternoon with friends or going on a three-hour shopping trip. I go for a fast walk or stroll through the park. Each time I come back refreshed and glad for my special kind of vacation.

God, sometimes the best I can do is get away for my mini-vacation. Thanks for providing that for me. Amen.

OF JAILS AND PRISONERS

"I'm in prison and I'm never, never going to get out," our daughter wailed. "I'm a prisoner of my own mind."

I offered her what comfort I could, reaffirming that her mother and I would always be with her.

In the months since then, I've thought of her words. She doesn't realize it, but we are prisoners too. We've had to act as jailers, keeping watch over her and giving her constant care. When she's been at her worst, we've made sure that she is never alone.

We received a heavy sentence too; as long as she's a prisoner of her mind, we're not free either. Deep within, we hope our parole will come. But until then we're determined to make the best of our private jail.

God, we can't escape this sentence and we accept that truth. Please enable us to accept our life without complaint, remembering that you don't make the load heavier than we can bear. Amen.

LETTING GO

"He can't live here." The doctor did not say "with you," but I felt the sting of the implication that we aren't a proper family. I saw my son's need to live elsewhere as evidence of my failure. I had let him down. No one actually accused me, but they didn't need to. I lived with self-accusations.

Three times my son had come home from the hospital and returned within weeks. I wanted him to get better, and I never consciously thwarted his progress. Yet our personalities are such that we made each other miserable.

If he is to improve, he will have to move into a kind of halfway house and from there on to independent living—all of this away from me.

While I outwardly agreed, inwardly I had not let go. I hurt because I felt self-accused. It took days of internal struggle before I said truthfully, "I want what's best for him." Then I let go.

God, he needs help, and yet I keep thinking mostly about my failure. Forgive me. Thank you for helping me let go. Amen.

REAL GUILT

I am guilty. I treated my wife badly for a long time. I screamed at her; I called her crazy; I threatened. "If you don't straighten up I'll have you put away and I'll see that you stay put away!" When she talked strangely, I felt scared.

I now understand I behaved the way I did because I was afraid. I didn't know what to do as her illness worsened. So I fought back the only way I knew how—with meanness and cruelty.

I don't do that any more, but I can't take back my words or undo my callous actions. I've apologized to her and she has forgiven me. I was wrong and felt the burden of guilt. I struggled with forgiving myself and am now learning about self-forgiveness.

Here's the prayer I find the most helpful:

Gracious God, Jesus pleaded for you to forgive his murderers because they didn't know what they were doing.* Forgive me, too, because I didn't know what I was doing to my wife. Amen.

---

*See Luke 23:34.

ONLY PEOPLE

I was scared, not knowing what to expect. I had seen TV programs about people who got out of mental institutions. Would he do something strange like one of them? If I said too much, would I upset him? If I kept quiet, would he think I didn't care? If I allowed his friends to visit, would they wear him out? If I urged them to stay away, would I make him a prisoner?

The doctor, aware of my anxiety, instructed me on how to relate to him. He said, "If you get confused about what to do or how to act around him, remember one thing: he's a person just like you. Ask yourself how you would want to be treated."

That bit of advice has helped me immensely. Inwardly I knew that principle, but I hadn't thought about applying it.

Loving God, Jesus told us to treat others the way we want to be treated,* and that rule hasn't changed. Thanks for reminding me. Amen.

---

*See Matthew 7:12.

MY TEACHER

After six weeks in the psychiatric hospital, our daughter has been undergoing therapy for a year.

Her doctors encouraged her to talk to me about feelings—all her feelings. One of them said, "For now, just feel, then talk about how you feel. Don't screen out what you think are bad emotions."

"That's fine for her," I told the doctor, "but I don't know how to listen. In our family we never talk about unpleasant things. In my childhood, my parents never allowed such talk."

"Then let her teach you," he said with a smile.

The thought repulsed me. *She's sick. She can't teach me anything.* But I was wrong. She has become my teacher. She has learned to be open about her emotions. In that regard, she's healthier than I am. I still find it hard to express anger or pain. But I'm determined to be a good pupil.

Teacher God, I'm grateful that she can help me while I try to help her. Don't let either of us give up. Amen.

BURNOUT

If the tears hadn't welled up, I might have laughed. The primary caseworker for our son resigned recently because of burnout. "Forty to fifty hours a week of pouring my soul out for these hurting people," she said. "I couldn't handle it any more."

After she left, in a moment of fantasy, I thought of resigning as the caring parent. "I'm burned out," I imagined saying to my son, "and I can't cope with you any more." Then reality hit again. I can't quit—and even though I occasionally want to, deep inside I know I could never leave him. He needs me. I suppose that's what keeps me away from total burnout.

I read once that all of us need to be needed. I get exhausted and overextended, but there's no giving up as long as he needs my love and my help.

God, you're always there for me, and you've given me a support group to lean on. Give me what I need to be always there for him. Amen.

SPIRITUAL FAILURE

The doctor told her, "You'll probably be on an antidepressant-antianxiety medication like Sinequan for a long time—possibly for the rest of your life."

At home she sobbed a long time. "I'm a spiritual failure. I always had faith in God and believed that God could do anything. But now—"

I held her, trying to comfort her in her pain and confusion. She's not a spiritual failure, and I hope that one day she will grasp that taking medicine means getting help, not failing—the way she would take medicine for a heart condition.

I want to reassure her, but right now my words seem meaningless. In time I hope she will see that Sinequan helps her to function each day.

God, thank you for providing medicine for our needs. Teach her and all others who require this kind of help that such drugs are your gifts to us. Amen.

TWO

CLARIFYING
THE FOCUS

SELF-ATTITUDE

"I'm no good," my husband muttered. "I can't work. I can't do anything for anybody." The words accompanied his neglect of his personal appearance.

As I prayed for wisdom in knowing what to say, a thought came to me: Because he doesn't feel good about who he is, he doesn't care how he looks. A second thought followed: If he looked better on the outside, he'd feel better on the inside. I gently insisted that he bathe, shave, and wear clean clothes. I frequently told him how nice he looked, pausing to touch or kiss him.

His improved appearance did pick up his spirits.

He had such low feelings of self-esteem that, by being dirty, he was trying to let me know how he really felt. I didn't cure him, but I helped him take care of his body, which enabled him to feel better about himself.

Holy God, I don't know if cleanliness is next to godliness, but I do know that when he's clean he feels better. Let us see his continued improvement. Amen.

PERFECT DAUGHTER

She was our perfect daughter—attractive, bright, athletic, well-groomed, and popular. Her grades hovered at the top of the class. It took her suicide attempt to wake us up.

"But why did you do this?" I pleaded.

After days of sullen silence, she said in a tiny voice, "I got tired of trying to be perfect."

She recounted the history of the demands she believed we had placed on her to surpass everyone. Even when she achieved, it wasn't good enough. She still felt pushed.

"I had no idea," I said limply. For several days I went through a time of self-examination. It did little good to say, "I didn't mean to be that way." I had wanted her to be the best. But I tried too hard. When we talked again, I said, "Forgive me. From now on, I only want you to be happy and to be nobody but the real you—however imperfect you are."

Wondrous God, you allowed me to become authentic. Help me allow her the same opportunity. Amen.

I HATE YOU

My son went into tantrums over little things and screamed obscenities at me. The worst came when he said calmly, "I hate you. You have ruined my life." To prevent my bursting into tears, I left the room.

A member of my support group suggested, "He may not mean what he said. He's probably saying he's frustrated. Or that he hates you for that one minute, not always."

"Or," said another, "maybe he's not been able to say things like that before; his language may be an emotional release."

When he now says, "I hate you," I react differently.

"I'm sorry you feel that way," I respond. I touch his hand or kiss his cheek. I want him to know that he can say those words to me and nothing will make me love him less. His freedom to express negative emotions may be necessary before he can articulate positive feelings toward me and others.

God, he's free to say what he feels even when I don't always like the words. Help me to accept him *even when I reject what he says. Amen.*

"IT'S YOUR FAULT"

"I've cut my wrists," she said, after having called me out of an important meeting, "and it's all your fault."

She repeated all the ways I had failed her for the last seven years. Such tactics had brought me racing home times before. This time I stayed at work. I said, "I hope you won't kill yourself; I love you."

She interrupted with fresh accusations and again added, "It's your fault."

"No, it's not my fault," I said, surprised at my own calmness. "I won't accept that responsibility." She had used this tactic before. She did not want to die; she needed reassurance of my concern. She also needed to accept responsibility for her own actions.

After hanging up, I wondered if I had done the right thing. What if she took her life? When I got home five hours later, I saw plastic tape over a tiny cut in each wrist. She hasn't threatened to take her life again, and I know I did the right thing.

Thank you, God, for giving me the strength to do what's right. We're both better now. Amen.

RESENTMENT

Unwisely I allowed him to alternate sleeping from twelve hours at a time to two. I ignored his angry outbursts and tolerated his talking jags. And somehow he got better—despite my foolish mistakes. When he came home from the hospital the second time, he said, "I want you to know that I'm holding a lot of resentment against you. You let me stay out of control."

My mistake had been lack of wisdom and insensitivity to his needs.

"I was sick," he said. "I couldn't do anything to stop myself, and I expected your help. I resented your not stopping me."

He has since enabled me to see the importance of my role as caregiver. I promised that if he ever went through phases like that again, I would lovingly intervene. I can help him more by not allowing bizarre behavior.

God, I failed and I'm sorry. He's forgiven me. Help me not to fail again when he needs me. Amen.

CRAZY LAUGHTER

Most of the time she did well at home. Once in a while when I was talking with someone else she would start what I call crazy laughter—a kind of cackling, forced laughing —and always at inappropriate times.

"Why did you do that?" I snapped back, angry at her rudeness. Each time she stopped, turned away, and refused to speak again for hours.

Her therapist suggested that I analyze what was going on when she started her crazy laugh. I soon noted that she interrupted when the conversation became strained, highly emotional, or argumentative.

Since then, I take people out of her hearing when we have to speak in emotion-charged terms. Or, when she is in the group, I have found that holding her hand or putting my arm around her makes her feel more secure, and she tends not to disrupt.

God, I concentrated too long on the displeasing behavior. Thank you for helping me to understand her real message. Amen.

ON ONE TRACK

His company fired him after fourteen years. He had been going downhill for a long time, and they kept him on the job for as long as they could.

After medical and psychological treatment, he's doing better. Each day he takes his medication, eats properly, and exercises. He still has one problem: his thoughts travel along one track, usually his old job, and nothing diverts him.

Unhindered, he will talk for hours, bringing up every unpleasant event in his fourteen-year history with the company. I have learned to say firmly, "That was the past. It's still sad to you, but we are going to think of the present and work toward a better future."

At first he argued, but now he realizes that staying on one track gets him no place. He wants to get better, and my intervention is one way I can help.

God, how thankful I am that you help us get beyond destructive and bitter memories! Keep reminding me of the bright future you have for both of us. Amen.

PRESSURES

"Why do you put this pressure on me all the time?" my daughter screamed.

In shock, I mumbled, "Because I want you to do well. It's for your own good."

"You think you're God! Always hassling me!"

Her words hurt, but afterward I thought about the charges. I *had* pressured her, thinking I was doing it for her own good. But was I?

With deep shame I admitted I had an inner image of what she ought to be and I pressured her to become that model child. Unintentionally, I had not allowed her to develop as herself.

"I was wrong," I said. "From now on I'll do my best to stop pressuring you."

When I forget and start to hassle her, she has a way of reminding me. She puts her palms together as if praying and says, "Yes, God." We both laugh. And I stop.

Wise God, forgive me when I try to control my daughter's life. Give me the wisdom to shut up. Amen.

ANGRY COMPLAINTS

After he spent three days in the hospital, I expected to see him recovering. Instead, I heard mostly complaints and angry outbursts.

"The food is rotten!

"The staff is lazy!

"Nobody comes when I need them!

"I'm tired of sleeping pills and needles!"

"You mustn't talk that way," I said. "You'll just upset yourself and get worse."

Now I realize I probably could not have said anything less helpful. But at the time, I assumed improving meant getting past anger and complaints. It took me a while to understand that he expressed nothing abnormal. Part of his healing came from his ability to talk about the kinds of feelings I wanted him to deny.

God, looking back I see that I did a lot of wrong things. As he learns to cope with everyday life, strengthen me so I can allow him to express his negative emotions. Amen.

TESTING

"I'm getting better," she said, "but what if I stop—exactly where I am now—and don't improve any more? Then what will you do about me?"

"I'll do just what I'm doing now," I answered. "I'll be with you."

I was slow at grasping what she was doing. Now I know that she was testing me, wanting to be sure that she could depend on me if she got bad again.

As long as she kept getting better, she knew I would be there. But she had to be sure I would not reject her if she got worse.

I encouraged her and commented on her progress, but most of all I assured her that I would stay with her whether she got better or not. "I'm with you, no matter what," I told her, "because I love you."

Faithful God, help me continue to give her the reassurance she needs that I'll always stay with her, just as you keep reminding me that you're always with me. Amen.

CONTROL

My husband fought hard and long to control everything in his life. He even got into a mind-control group, insisting that he could use the power of his mind to direct the actions of others.

Sadly, I realized it was his fear of powerlessness that kept him grasping and pushing for mastery. He had, at best, a tenuous grasp on the circumstances of his own life, and so he tried to dominate everything.

One day, as he himself said, "I stretched the rubber band a little too far. I tried too hard to keep control."

No matter how well he gets, his fear of helplessness is there. Much of his problem stems from unresolved childhood dilemmas. Because I can understand his great need, I am more understanding and far more patient.

God, we all want to control the events of our lives. He feels this need more than most. Help him release his grasping for control and trust you more. Amen.

GOING BACKWARD

Always a meticulous person, she changed drastically. She became unkempt, wore the same clothes for days, and wouldn't bathe or brush her teeth. Then gradually she pulled out of her depression. But a year later she again started to neglect her personal hygiene.

"Have you thought," asked a friend who was caregiver for a forty-year-old son, "that, because of internal stress and confusion, she's regressing to an earlier stage in life when someone else took care of her—a time of security?"

His words made sense and helped me to cope better. Without demanding, I ran her bath and escorted her to the tub. While she washed, I laid out fresh clothes. I handed her a comb and she fixed her hair. Placing the toothpaste and brush on the washbasin was usually all it took for her to brush her teeth.

When she goes through a regressive period, I now know a little better how to cope.

Parent God, make me more sensitive to her needs and understanding of her regressions. Amen.

THE CAUSE

He slept only two or three hours at a time; he moved constantly and talked incessantly. At 3:00 A.M. he decided to repair the back steps. I kept silent, ignoring his strangeness, determined to stay calm. Eventually, my anger exploded. "You may get a lot of pleasure out of never sleeping and all this moving around, but I can't stand any more. Stop doing it!"

I'll never forget his pained expression. "I wouldn't do it if I could stop," he said.

I had gotten so upset over the action I never thought of the cause.

"We'll work it out together," I said. And we are finding ways, because I can now look at the symptoms and not the actions.

God, I'm thankful that you always know what's in my heart and don't judge me on the basis of my actions. Help me to do the same for him. Amen.

HYPERACTIVE

Before she went to the hospital, she didn't want to do anything but sleep. She stayed in bed sixteen hours at a time. When she came back, she didn't want to sleep. After two or three hours she seemed charged up and filled with energy. She wore me out. She started on talking jags, rambling from one topic to another. Or she paced the house, as if she had to continue on the move every moment.

I took it as long as I could, and then I called my sister to come over. I had to get away from her or crack up myself. I know that telling her to stop pacing and be calm and sit quietly won't stop her hyperactivity. She can't help doing what she's doing.

Her doctor says that eventually she will settle down and won't be so hyper all the time. As long as she'll pull out of it eventually, I can put up with it—or get someone else to come in when I can't.

God, remind me that her hyperactivity is normal behavior as she is now. Amen.

OPPRESSIVE SILENCE

When he came home from the hospital, he wouldn't speak except to say yes or no. I coaxed, cajoled, and tried to trick him into talking, but he remained adamant. He wouldn't (or couldn't) tell me why. I had never realized until then the oppressiveness of silence. He didn't want the TV on and wouldn't let me play the stereo.

The doctor allayed my worries. "If he doesn't want to talk, respect that right. He'll talk when he's ready or when he has something to say. You go ahead and live your life."

Once in a while he'll talk for a few minutes or an hour. Then silence will prevail for days. But I'm more comfortable with it now, and I no longer find his silence oppressive.

God, I don't enjoy the noiselessness but at least I can tolerate it. Help me to respect his need for silence. Amen.

DEPRESSIVE FEELINGS

I'd always heard, "Let people talk about their feelings. Help them get everything out." In her case, it didn't help. She was depressed, and the more she talked about it, the deeper she sank. "I'm no good to you or anybody. I want to die," she'd repeat.

When I discussed it with the doctor, he said, "Concentrate on facts and everyday events. Don't deny feelings but don't dwell on them. She's been carrying around an overload of feelings and needs to get away from them for a while. Let her."

He gave me sound advice. I concentrated on making her comfortable and focused on daily events. Weeks went by before she said, "I still feel awful, but I don't want to die any more."

That was the first concrete encouragement I had from her. Now I know I must learn when to urge her to talk about feelings and when to avoid such talk.

God, thank you for giving me wisdom through the therapist. Help me to remain sensitive to her needs. Amen.

SUSPICIOUS

"She doesn't like me," he said of my best friend. "I can tell by the look in her eyes." By then I realized he had become suspicious of everyone.

The first few times he expressed distrust I tried to talk him out of such feelings. "She's fond of you, dear. Why, she'd do anything for you." My words never convinced him and only worsened the situation.

"Why do you insist so much?" he charged. "You're trying to protect those people, but I know how they really feel."

I finally figured out that he needed emotional distance from people. He got this privacy by being suspicious of their actions and motives. Without being aware of his actions, he used accusations and fearfulness about their motives to back away from everyone.

God, help me to understand what's going on inside him and to respond to his need and not try to change him through empty words. Amen.

THREATS

"Once in a while she gets stubborn, we argue, then she makes threats."

"What kind of threats?" the doctor asked.

"That she'll do away with herself. That she'll leave the house and never come back."

"Don't take her threats lightly," he said. "At the same time, you don't help any by letting her manipulate you."

After helping me to understand how my daughter played on my fears, the doctor suggested ways for me to respond.

Yesterday my daughter didn't want to take her medicine. "I'll get a lot of pills," she threatened, "and swallow all of them at one time, and then I'll die."

"You need these two tablets," I said. "I'd like you to take them. When you make threats, you scare me and I wish you wouldn't do that. But threats or no threats, you need these pills." She took them with no further resistance.

Loving God, her manipulative threats still scare me. Give me wisdom to cope with these bad moments. Amen.

BEING DIFFERENT

He felt different—and he says that all his life he has felt different from other people. In some sense I suppose we've all felt the same way at times.

But his awareness went far deeper. Emotionally he translated *different* to equal *bad* or *sinful.*

I don't want to try to talk him out of these feelings (I couldn't anyway). Through the suggestions of my support group, I am now saying things to him like, "Perhaps you do feel stronger about things or react more sensitively than many of us. Such feelings don't make you bad. This awareness means that your feelings are not the same—nothing else."

He's making slow progress in accepting that it is all right to be different and that being different brings no negative judgment.

Divine Teacher, help him to learn that it is all right to feel different. Help me to allow him that difference. Amen.

HOW COULD YOU?

Grandfather raced into the room and stared at her weary body under the white covers. "How could you do such a thing to us?"

I wanted to stop him and protect my sister but I didn't know what to say. I also had felt some humiliation over her attempted suicide. We live in a small town, and now everyone knows what happened. Yet I also understood that I had to look beyond my own feelings. I said, "Grandpa, she's hurting inside. It was the only way she knew to stop hurting."

"Nonsense! She could have talked to me! Or seen a doctor! Or our pastor!" His anger didn't subside, and he never moved beyond the how-could-you? stage.

After he left I said, "Sis, I understand a little better now why you did it. I didn't realize how much you had to put up with. And I'm sorry for Grandpa's words."

Sis squeezed my hand. And from then on we became true friends.

Compassionate God, my sister has a lot of pain and I care. Thank you for making me aware of more than my own pain. Amen.

THREE

OTHERS
IN FOCUS

NETWORK THERAPY

We developed network therapy from a series of three meetings. It worked like this: We invited everybody who we thought might be of help. This included relatives, former neighbors, my husband's friends from grade school, even his barber. I told them his whole history, not exaggerating and not holding back. They asked questions and spoke of their own feelings and concerns.

At the third meeting we said, "Those who want to help—in any way—here is your chance to volunteer." And they responded.

One man picks him up for church, another brings him home. He has lunch every week with a third person. One man comes over regularly and they view vintage films on the VCR. Five others formed a crisis team— people who are available for emergencies. These friends have stood by him for more than two years. He has not had a serious setback since he began the network therapy.

God, thank you for a therapy network— your hands reaching out to help. Amen.

WOUNDED LOVERS

I read about a family with twin boys, both schizophrenics. I phoned to offer my sympathy and said, "I know some of your pain. I have a mentally ill daughter."

We talked for two hours, interspersing words with tears. I acquired a new friend—another person who knows the depth of pain that caregivers of the mentally ill experience. She's a wounded lover like me, a caregiver who has experienced painful reactions and rejections from the object of her love, yet still commits to loving.

Since she belongs to a local support group, she invited me to go with her. I started to attend meetings, and soon I found other wounded lovers. We have bonded in our common needs and commitments.

Finding wounded lovers has given me a new perspective and added strength for the battles of daily living.

God, you found me a long time ago, and now you have enabled me to find others that I can reach out to. You made them easy to find because their hands were already stretched toward me. Amen.

FAMILY DOCTORS

I have no medical degree but in many ways I have become his doctor—and so has the whole family. We're not unusual. About 65 percent of mental patients now return to their families, usually their parents. And we have to learn to cope with him and his problems.

And we did learn! Sometimes we make mistakes. We wonder about our own mental health. But we do what we can. We are a family, and we provide the nursing and social network.

"How do you do it?" a friend asked. "The demands on your life seem so great."

"I don't know," I answered truthfully, "but I turn to God for strength and the rest of the family for encouragement. My reward comes when I see our son's smile or when he goes to sleep at night, contented and peaceful."

God, friends tell me I do so much; I thank you for what I can do. I love him, and I know your parental heart understands. Amen.

SOMETHING SPECIAL

When I was growing up, our neighbors had a retarded baby who never learned to walk or talk. I used to feel sorry for them, and one day I told the mother about my concern.

"Thank you," she said. "Some days are hard." Her eyes filled with tears as she added, "But we also have something special. Our little Patty has brought a love into our home that we would never have known otherwise."

I didn't understand her then; now I have had the same experience. Our daughter is twenty-one, and she is mentally ill. Her condition demands so much time and energy that some nights I fall across the bed, too tired to undress.

Some days are hard. Yet, like that mother, I know our daughter has brought something special into our home: a deeper compassion for hurting people, a greater sensitivity to needs.

God, despite all the hardship, thank you for giving her to us as a special gift. Amen.

DOUBLE TROUBLE

Many people don't understand the double effect mental illness has on the family.

First, the emotional drain: We must constantly watch over him, doing what we can, trying to relieve stress and to express our loving care. That means a constant drain of energy, and sometimes we barely hold on.

Second, the financial drain: They diagnosed my husband as schizophrenic when he was twenty-three, and he is now thirty-one. Despite a good income, we're heavily in debt and envision no future relief.

"How do you handle it?" a friend asked. "I could handle either the sickness or the financial stress, but I couldn't do both."

"You handle what you have to," I said. "I didn't choose this way of life, but I do have a network of friends, sympathetic doctors, and a faith in God that keeps me going."

God, what would I do without you and the helping people you send into my life? Thank you for your strength. Amen.

CALLING FOR HELP

My wife started screaming abusively. She threw everything from dishes to small items of furniture at me. Then she locked herself inside the bedroom and screamed that she was going to kill me and then herself. I pleaded with her for almost an hour before I phoned for help.

It embarrassed me to call the police and ask them to come, but I had to do something. They parked in front of our house; the neighbors walked back and forth, trying to see inside. I was too ashamed to go out and see them.

A policewoman talked to her through the closed door for a long time before my wife came out. As they left the police said, "You'd better call your own doctor." In that moment, I realized that embarrassment over phoning for help was not nearly as important as responding to my wife's need.

God, forgive me for thinking only of me when she's hurting. I want her well; help me to do everything I can to assist in that process. Amen.

CHEATING

For more than a year our family kept Dad's mental problems a secret. We all agreed that we didn't want a lot of nosy questions asked.

Since Dad already had physical problems, it made it easier for us to cover up his mental illness. For more than a year, we kept it our secret.

In a conversation with my Sunday school teacher the truth slipped out and I began to apologize for bringing up our problem.

"You should apologize! You have cheated us—all of your church friends. The church is a family. We share each other's burdens and joys. If you don't tell us and you insist on handling troubles alone, you are cheating us out of the opportunity of active caring."

I realized he was right. Had the roles been reversed, I would have wanted the opportunity to express my love and concern.

God, you care, but sometimes I forget that people can care too. Help me not to cheat them again. Amen.

NOT ALONE

Aside from her illness, coping with being alone has proven to be the hardest thing I face. For a long time I didn't know anyone else who cared for a mentally ill family member.

Periodically, self-pity struck and I'd hear myself saying, "I can't talk to other people because nobody else understands what I go through."

In the hospital waiting room, I met another man my age, also a caregiver. But he had outside support. He told me about NAMI—the National Alliance for the Mentally Ill—and two other organizations, Emotions Anonymous and Recovery, Inc.* That week I joined a support group, and for the first time I am with others who have also experienced pain, loss, shame, and guilt. They understand me and have given me comfort, support, and friendship.

God, I'm never alone with you in my life, and yet I felt that way. Thank you for these groups of people who care. Amen.

---

*See list of addresses at the back of this book.

VALUED IMPERFECTIONS

I never thought I would say, "I like being imperfect," but now I say it *and mean it.* I tried so hard to be the perfect friend— everything to everybody. I dared not make mistakes or people wouldn't like me. I played superwoman at work and super-mom at home. I refused to settle for mediocrity or letting anything be only "good enough."

One Sunday our pastor preached on Jesus' statement "There is only One who is good"* and pointed out the wrongness of an unhealthy striving for perfection. (He called it sin.) "If you could be perfect, you wouldn't need God's help," he said. "Look at your failures and shortcomings," he said. "Value your imperfections. Then you can turn to God for help."

Flawless and holy God, because I can now value my imperfections, I am aware of how much I need you. Help me as I try to care for him with his problems. We're both imperfect people who need wisdom and strength. Amen.

---

*Matthew 19:17, NIV.

UNDERSTANDING FRIENDS

Before our daughter became noticeably ill, she had many friends, involved herself in school activities, and regularly attended parties and sports events. After her treatment, I didn't want her to go out socially again for a long time. Her friends didn't understand at first what had happened in her life. The same friends phoned or visited, but several of them treated her differently. Some talked to her as if she had become retarded.

One girlfriend, in my daughter's presence, asked me, "She isn't violent, is she?"

Another asked, "Can she dress herself?"

I told both of them, "Why don't you ask her?"

Fortunately, not all her friends act so insensitively. Most of them understand that she was ill and is now better. By their caring they are assisting her continued improvement.

Compassionate God, thank you for the love of her friends. Remind me that even the foolish ones mean well. Amen.

MAGIC NUMBER

Once again I had told my support group the pain his mental problems cause me. The intense level of my words surprised me because I hadn't grasped that I needed to talk more about him.

"Listen," a member of the group said and read one sentence from a book: "Perhaps there's a magic number—like thirty-seven times—that the story has to be verbalized before a catharsis takes place."*

I hesitated; I had mentioned the same incidents before and told of my own pain. Yet I sensed my need to say it all again, for what must have been the tenth time. As I finished, a strange calmness came over me. Then I knew: the pain and anger had gone. I didn't have to wait until the magic number 37; my healing came at number 10.

God, thank you for friends who listen—really listen—so that hurting people like me can reach their own magic number and find healing. Amen.

*Cecil Murphey, *Comforting Those Who Grieve* (Atlanta: John Knox Press, 1979), p. 30.

DRAINING OFF

"Have you drained off your feelings?" a friend asked. "You have to deal with *you* before you can deal with *her* again."

I didn't understand, but he wouldn't let me go until I did.

"Draining off means going through each incident that caused you pain. Talk about your hurt with someone you trust. Let the anger, or whatever feelings you have, spill out. Otherwise your emotions remain like a volcano ready to explode."

Right then he let me drain off on him. I admitted my anger, my pain, my embarrassment, my sorrow, and all the other held-back emotions. I didn't totally calm the tumult, but I made a start. By talking in a safe environment and allowing my raw emotions to emerge, I drained them of their power.

God, I've drained off my pain. Now help me rebuild my life while she's getting better. Amen.

THE SAFE PLACE

Between his constant dependence on me and the children's having different needs for me to respond to, I felt trapped. I had to be strong for everybody.

And I was strong for ten months, not giving way to tears or allowing myself to get discouraged.

But last week in our self-help group, I couldn't keep it up; I broke down and wept. I couldn't hold back the tears, even though I tried. The group propped me up emotionally and gave me the compassion I needed.

When I tried to apologize for my tears, one of them said, "This is the place to cry or yell or whatever you need to do. We provide a safe place for you here. This is the safe place for all of us. You don't need to apologize, and we hope you'll overcome your embarrassment."

God, thank you for my safe place with those special people who care. They reflect your compassion for me. Amen.

FOUR

FOCUS
ON CARING

PROMISE LITTLE

She was better and I wanted her to get completely well. I was ready to do anything I could to help. I talked with her doctor, who gave me sage advice: "Promise little; do much."

Later, one of her friends assured me, "I'll drop in to see her every week."

"Don't promise," I said. "Visit, but don't feel guilty if you can't come."

The friend came faithfully for several weeks before she skipped a week . . . then two weeks. Three months have passed since her last visit. My wife misses her friend's visits, and so do I. But I'm glad I wouldn't let her friend make a promise—and then break it.

I've also stopped myself from overpromising. I want to reassure her, to be available when needed, but I refuse to overcommit. In the long run that's better for both of us.

God, you're the only one whose promises never fail. Thank you that we can rely on your faithfulness. Strengthen me so that I truly promise little but do much. Amen.

CRAZY

I couldn't understand his strange behavior and tried to figure him out.

"I'm crazy," he said. "Just plain crazy." He gestured toward the others in the room. "We're all crazy here."

"Don't say such a thing!" I admonished.

"It's true," he said. "And when you can talk that way you find it shows you're not afraid any more. We're sick, and sometimes laughing about it helps us not to cry over things we can't control."

Then he said, "Don't worry about my craziness. I'm not going to stay this way. I figured out that I needed to go crazy as my first step toward health."

I understood: only by giving in to his confusion and inner pain could he reach out for help.

He *is* sick—crazy—and needs treatment. But we both know he is going to get better.

God, I'll never understand all his craziness but I love him. I'm with him, no matter what. Give me the strength to carry out my commitment. Amen.

ONLY ONCE

So far as we could tell, she had never had symptoms of mental illness. Then, like some-one waking up with a cold, one morning she complained about the television set broadcasting her thoughts to the whole world. She wouldn't go to her college classes because "everyone whispers about me."

We got help for our daughter immediately. Within months the symptoms disappeared. Now, four years later, she has had no further trouble. Our doctor termed it *reactive schizophrenia.* "Her illness began with one intensely painful dilemma. This has now cleared up," he said. "She shows no further serious problems."

"Are you sure?" I asked.

"No one can be sure," he said. "But we live with hope."

Even though we still have a slight fear, we live in expectancy. She became sick once. And we expect it to be only once.

God, she has been symptom-free for four years. Give us greater peace so we can be symptom-free too. Amen.

INVOLUNTARY COMMITMENT

Our son progressed well for eighteen months. Slowly the old symptoms started to reappear. We warned him and urged him to get help. "I'm doing fine," he always said.

But he wasn't fine; the bizarre behavior patterns recurred. Our only recourse was involuntary commitment. In our state we had to go to court and explain to the judge about his psychotic relapse and his refusal to acknowledge his condition.

We felt grossly humiliated by the entire courtroom scene. Among strangers, we had to prove that he posed a danger to himself and to others and needed temporary hospitalization. In telling of his dangerous behavior, we felt the stigma of shame as if we had caused or exacerbated his problems.

We won in court—or did we? The decision affects us as deeply as it does our son.

God, we too have been involuntarily committed, and this realization hurts; we feel alone in our pain. Bring us the comfort and peace that only you can provide. Amen.

ONE WORD

I left the hospital in a state of rage. They had her so medicated that she hardly made sense when she tried to talk. One word came to me: zombie.

The next day I demanded a meeting with her doctor. "I want you to cut out all that medicine that keeps her doped up." He listened patiently and then summarized her condition with one word that made me reconsider: overwhelmed.

"I'd like you to remember it," he said. "That word expresses her emotional state right now. She has had such a flood of emotions that the impact crushed her. We sedated her heavily— temporarily—to give her time and to help pull her out from under the overwhelming load. For right now that level of medication is necessary."

"I never thought of it like that," I said.

God, I still don't like seeing her in a drugged state. Help me to understand that, for now, *she needs to get away from those problems and emotions. Amen.*

PPD

"Some patients suffer from PPD—post-psychotic depression—after they return home," his new doctor cautioned, after the third hospitalization. "Be aware and be understanding."

After his first two hospitalizations—both lasting several weeks—we didn't understand PPD and weren't as helpful as we might have been. When he started to show signs of depression, we pushed the PANIC button. We did not consider that his depressive response might be quite normal.

This time, within a month after coming home, he went into depression. We showered him with extra attention, reminding him that he could go back to the hospital if he needed to. Slowly he pulled out of the despondency.

We hope he won't need hospitalization again, but we've learned to watch for PPD—and to be there with loving assurance and great patience.

God, some of us learn slowly. But thank you that we do learn. Amen.

ECT

When we heard the proper term, *electric convulsive therapy,* we quickly translated that to *shock treatment* and felt scared. We had heard too many horror stories and seen too many depictions on TV programs. Her doctor eased our concern by making several points:

- ECT is used only with selected patients
- ECT is most effective on people forty-five to fifty-five with no previous history of depression
- Patients have a minimal (usually temporary) loss of memory
- Patients tend to sleep deeply afterward

She had been sleeping fitfully; she dwelt constantly on the past. Because she was a carefully screened patient, the ECT treatment brought an immediate improvement.

God, we get scared about terms and types of treatment. Give us courage and wisdom as we explore the ways that will best help her and others in need. Amen.

DRUG EDUCATION

When he became ill I didn't know anything about drugs. I learned that drug therapy is now used far more than psychological help alone. Many doctors know that mentally ill patients have chemical imbalances. Autopsies have shown that both the architecture and the chemistry of their brains can be different from normal people.

As caregivers we soon learned that medication for psychiatric illness comes in three classifications: *antipsychotics* or *neuroleptics* (used for those with hallucinations and delusions), *antidepressants,* and *antianxiety* drugs.

I'm thankful the doctor explained so much because I shuddered when she first told me our son "would probably be on medication the rest of his life."

Now that I understand, I accept his need for drugs, and I'm glad they are available.

God, how wonderfully you have provided medicine to make up for natural deficiencies. Thank you for medical breakthroughs. Amen.

TARDIVE DYSKINESIA

The speaking of those two words sounded like the seal of judgment upon my wife: tardive dyskinesia—involuntary physical movements that are side effects from drugs. When the doctors started her treatment program they told us only 13 percent have this side effect. Unfortunately, she fell into that category.

Her tardive dyskinesia involves the tongue—it darts in and out. The action causes no harm. Yet watching this now-habitual action tears me apart emotionally. I want her free from this side effect. At the same time, I remember only too well her odd behavior and deep depressions before treatment. At least she now works part-time, has few drastic mood swings, and is more pleasant to be around.

God, when I focus on her unsettling side effects and feel sad, remind me that she is better. And because I want to see her completely well, I pray for that now and every day. Amen.

DID I?

He's been taking an antipsychotic drug under the brand name of Thorazine. About a month lapsed before we saw much change, but since then he has continued to improve.

He is so aware of his dependence on Thorazine that it creates one problem for him. "Did I take it today?" I've heard him ask himself. "I can't remember."

When not sure he tended to take another, and that could lead to overdosing. Because many of these drugs are cumulative, patients often feel no effect from missing one or two days.

When I realized how deeply this troubled him, I bought a plastic pillbox with a compartment for each day of the week, clearly labeled. Each Sunday he fills the box for the week. If the space for Tuesday is empty, he knows he has taken the pill.

"That relieves my anxiety," he said, "although I sometimes have to check it two or three times a day to make sure."

God, thank you for simple solutions to the problems that plague us each day. Amen.

HOSPITAL FREE

The news excited me, and when I told her she said, "Oh, that's fine," although her voice lacked enthusiasm.

My wife had gone through a severe and prolonged depression and voluntarily admitted herself for treatment. After seven weeks she became an outpatient, going back to the hospital every day for medicine and therapy. As she continued to improve, they cut her return trips to four days a week, then to three, and finally to just one day. Then came the good news: she would not have to return.

She was home two days before I grasped why she took the news badly. She believed the doctor no longer wanted to treat her. She felt abandoned.

"You can go back to the hospital," I assured her, "anytime *you* need to." Now that she understands, she rejoices with me in her successful treatment.

God, so often we misinterpret out of fear and uncertainty. Reassure both of us about your ongoing presence in our lives. Amen.

CONVALESCENCE

On the day of his release, we joyfully told him the plans we had made. "We've arranged for you to reenter the spring quarter at college. You have your part-time job back." Two of his friends had arranged welcome-home parties.

"I'd suggest you not make any immediate plans for him," the caseworker said.

"But he's doing better, and—"

"He may not be ready for a lot of activity," she insisted. "If he had undergone major surgery, wouldn't you give him time to recuperate? Think of this in the same way."

We brought him home and put *our* plans on hold. The caseworker was right. He needed to readjust to fit in again. He didn't know if his friends really wanted to see him. For two weeks he stayed inside the house. Then he said, "I want to go to church Sunday." That event began his reentry into the world.

God, thank you for the wisdom you impart to us through others. Amen.

SURVIVING

Diagnosed as schizophrenic, Edna (not her real name) underwent hospitalization nine times and was medicated with eighteen different drugs over an eleven-year period. She told me her history and concluded, "I had no one with me, yet I survived."

Edna told me of others who had taken their own lives, of those who didn't want to get better. "But I survived," she said again.

My wife wasn't sick then—or at least we didn't recognize the symptoms.

Recently I told a friend about my wife's ordeal with mental illness and heard myself saying, "but she survived." Then I remembered Edna's having said the same thing about herself.

Yes, my wife is a survivor too. And she has one special factor in her life that Edna didn't have—my wife has me by her side.

God, I'm grateful that my wife is surviving. She's also recovering, and that makes me even more thankful. Amen.

TAKING A CHANCE

He had been cruel to the children and brutal to me. He hadn't spoken a loving word to us in the past five years. When the physical violence erupted, I demanded that he get help. The doctor thought his condition was serious enough for a lengthy hospitalization.

Free of immediate pressure, I had time to think of the children and my own future. I decided this would be the perfect time to divorce him—when I would not have to fear his violent response.

On the next visit, I told him. He said, "I don't want to be this way. I love you and I want to get well."

Then I knew I couldn't desert him—much as I wanted to. I won't leave as long as there is a chance. I can't say that I still love him, but I married him and promised to stay with him until death. Now I have hope—only a glimmer, but enough to take a chance on.

God, you never gave up on me, and I don't want to give up on him. Help me to keep that determination. Amen.

LONG-SUFFERING

"Haven't I suffered enough? Haven't I put up with her craziness for years? How much more does God expect of me?"

"How much more do you expect of yourself?" my pastor asked. "Only you and God know how much you can take. It's up to you."

I had expected him to tell me that I must stay with her no matter what. I had anticipated that he would remind me of my wedding vows. I was prepared to argue with him. When he left it up to me, all my defenses collapsed. The decision was mine to make.

I prayed for guidance, and that day I understood the meaning of faith. Faith means hanging on when we have nothing to assure us that life will turn out right. Faith won't let go in the midst of pain and confusion. Faith is the willingness to suffer long.

God, I'm depending on you to help me in my long-suffering so I can keep holding on. And you know, God, I believe I can—with your help. Amen.

TREATMENT

"Surely you have some kind of drug to cure my husband!" I cited examples of the medical progress in the past thirty years.

"We don't know the cause of mental illness," the doctor said. "Until we do, we can't design the proper drug treatment. At best we hope to control his behavior."

The doctor prescribed lithium carbonate, a drug used since the early 1950s. "It has a powerful mood-stabilizing effect and can be used safely," he said. "Lithium prevents high and low mood extremes."

I wish the doctor had given me a more optimistic picture. My husband's daily lithium doses have caused his manic attacks to occur less frequently, and even when they recur, they are less severe.

While I still hope for a total cure, at least he has relief. Lithium isn't a perfect medicine, but for families like us, these drugs keep our loved ones functioning.

God, until you give researchers the cure for mental illness, make us thankful for what we have. Amen.

PROTECTIVE INSTINCTS

She's gone through a lot already, I reasoned. She doesn't need any more pain. I began to protect her from anything I thought would upset her. I cautioned visitors in advance; I held back a few letters; I selected TV programs and censored magazines. I thought I was making her stronger.

"Your protectiveness is understandable," a friend said, "just not very helpful." He enabled me to realize that, as much as I didn't want her to be troubled, I couldn't shield her from life's hardships. Part of living involves facing pain, rejection, disappointment, and misunderstanding.

I've found a better way for my protective instincts to work. I no longer insulate her, and I'm there to remind her that life isn't always fair. I wrap my arms around her when she hits the rough edges of life. "I care," I say, and she believes me.

Parent God, I want her to grow strong. Give me wisdom so that I don't insulate her from life and actually hurt her more. Amen.

PUNISHING

At first I let him dwell on his self-doubts. He could go on endlessly repeating how bad he was and saying that if I had any brains I would divorce him.

After I learned that I didn't help him by encouraging such self-denigration, I said, "I will not listen to you brood aloud on your failures. You are not a failure."

"If you won't talk about what I want to talk about," he said, "I won't say anything to you." He turned away and refused to speak to me for the rest of that day and for a whole week.

I almost gave in, until I realized he was punishing me for not helping him get worse. I didn't like the silence and I didn't have to tolerate it. I turned on the TV; I hummed quietly. One day I read aloud, not sure if he listened.

He constantly stared at me, anger blazing in his eyes. On the eighth day he spoke to me—only a few sentences, but he had begun.

God, thank you for your help in winning this battle. I now see that my persistence means we both won. Amen.

REWARDING MISERY

"I feel so bad, putting you through this," she said. "I've failed you in everything I've ever done. Why do you put up with it? How can you stay with a loser like me?"

For several days I listened, sometimes for hours, while she droned on, recounting every mistake she had made since childhood. Although I didn't recognize the effects of my action then, I was actually rewarding her misery. By letting her focus on self-loathing, I reinforced her words.

At the suggestion of her therapist, I have stopped asking how she feels. I don't give her a chance to parade her misery because it leads her into deeper despair. Instead I talk about events and places and people. We are both learning macramé, and we're doing handwork together to give away as presents at Christmas.

God, I care deeply about her. I want her to get better, so don't let me reward her misery by listening to all the painful details of failure. Amen.

TALKING ABOUT IT

I've always heard that talking about problems makes them easier to handle. I tried the idea out on him. "Just talk to me about how you feel," I pleaded. "Get it out of your system."

"I don't want to," he said.

No matter how hard I tried or how I maneuvered the conversation around to talking about emotions, he wouldn't open up.

In desperation I went to my support group and told them my story. One man said, "Ever try to talk to a drowning person? Talking isn't important then. Saving him is what counts."

Something clicked for me. He doesn't have to talk about how he feels. Instead of helping, I may have hindered his progress. Today I just said, "If you ever get ready to talk about anything, I'll be here."

Wise God, you have a time for all things in life. Help me to respect his right not to talk. Amen.

FORCING

She came home from the hospital with greasy, stringy hair. I waited a week before I said, "Your hair's filthy."

"I don't care," she said.

I demanded that she wash her hair and she refused. I tried shaming her. "What will our friends think if they see you looking that way?"

"They don't have to see me," she said.

I tried everything except hitting her. Nothing worked. In desperation I called a member of my support group, who told me, "You've tried all the wrong ways. Now do it the smart way. Run the water for her. Say gently, 'I'd like you to wash your hair.' Act as if you expect cooperation. If she still refuses, wait and try it again the next day."

Her advice paid off. We still have problems, but I've determined that I won't make demands or use force.

Caring God, you help without forcing your will upon us. Strengthen me so that I can treat her in the same loving manner. Amen.

HUMORING

He nearly drove me into a psychiatric hospital with his constant talking. From the time he got up until I finally got him into bed, he rambled on and on. He kept throwing out ideas that would earn him a million dollars and went on endlessly telling me all the details.

I let him ramble on. But by humoring him, I ended up depressed and almost dysfunctional. That's when I realized that, for both our sakes, I couldn't humor him any more.

From his therapist I picked up four practical tips: (1) I say, "Slow down, you're talking too fast," and I make sure he slows down. (2) I say, "Wait. Breathe deeply five times. You're getting pretty excited, and this will calm you a little." (3) Occasionally I divert his attention with a new topic. (4) I follow two rules when he gets overactive—I will not humor him, and I will act in kindness and not anger.

God, thank you for enabling me to help him more effectively. Amen.

WATCHING

After she came home she spent most of the first week in bed. I constantly tiptoed in to check on her. When I went to work I insisted that she call me every hour. From the time I got home until bedtime, I devoted my attention to her.

But I paid a price. My job suffered; I became irritable; our relationship deteriorated.

"Why do you keep watching me all the time?" she asked.

"Because I care about you," I said, "and want to be sure you're all right."

"You're afraid," she said. "You're afraid I'm going to crack up again."

She was right, although I didn't want to admit the truth. Yet she could tell.

"I don't want to go through that again," she said. "But if I do, I won't go off the deep end in two hours. Give yourself a break. Spend a little time caring about yourself."

For once, I took *her* advice!

God, watch over her as only you can. Keep me calmly trusting you. Amen.

"LEAVE ME ALONE"

He kept insisting, "Just let me stay by my-self." I was reluctant to do that. He had tried to kill himself on two previous occasions—both of them after periods of withdrawal.

He again withdrew from all physical activity. He spent hours staring out the window. He lost interest in conversation. "I'd like to be alone so I can think," he said.

A member of my support group said, "When they're deeply depressed, don't leave them alone. People seldom take their own lives when others are around."

For three weeks I made sure that he was never alone, despite his caustic objections and ver-bal demands. On his next appointment I told the doctor of my concerns, and she agreed I had done the right thing.

God, sometimes we have to do things we don't like because it's for another person's good. Remind me of that the next time I complain about your activities in my own life. Amen.

PRIVATE SPACE

When our daughter came home after treatment, we were afraid to leave her alone even though she had done nothing violent or self-destructive. We tried to be with her every moment. Someone was available to drive her to and from college or anywhere else.

One day she went on a yelling rampage—one of the first serious signs we had detected before her hospitalization. My heart sank as I thought of the gloomy future.

"Just let me alone! I am not a puppy you need to keep on a leash," she said.

"What do you want?" I asked, keeping my voice calm.

"I want private space where I can be alone to think things through by myself. You make me feel like a prisoner here."

With reluctance we gave her privacy—exactly what our daughter needed. Her attitude improved, and I soon saw her smiling again.

God, she does need private space. Forgive us for being too protective. Guide us in knowing how to respond lovingly. Amen.

FOR HIS OWN GOOD

We kept secrets from him, such as not telling him why his sister wouldn't visit. All for his own good, I reasoned. Because I thought he couldn't handle the information, I withheld it. Later he found out she was afraid that "I might go crazy if I get around him."

My actions made him suspicious and distrustful. They tore down his self-confidence at a time when he badly needed to believe in himself. Too late I realized that I could have found a way to tell him about his sister's attitude.

While I kept telling myself, I'm doing this for his good, I now wonder. Was I acting for his good or mine? Was it because *I* couldn't handle his pain? I'm not totally sure, but I have promised that I will not withhold information, no matter how painful for either of us. In the long run, that's best for him—and for me.

God, by wanting to protect him from hurt, I caused more pain. Give me greater wisdom. Amen.

SOCIAL PACE

Before her illness became severe, she had immersed herself in countless activities—which may have exacerbated the already-present problem.

After her hospitalization, I told her, "Take as long as you need to get involved. I'll step in if I see you getting too entangled."

I said those words when she was afraid to mingle with people again. I didn't push, but I gently nudged her to set a date when she would go to church with me.

The first Sunday, we arrived a little late and sat on the aisle in the back row. Not many people saw her. As soon as the service finished, she hurried outside. It took weeks before she talked to anyone after service. One day she said, "I want to go back to Sunday school."

That was the day I had waited for. By starting at a slow pace, she moved back into activities as she was ready. She now enjoys life more than ever.

God, she's happy, and that makes me feel happy. Guide her as she moves at the right pace—her pace. Amen.

THE BAD NEWS

My husband's brother lost his job and walked out on his wife. Should I tell my husband? I wondered.

Family members urged me not to upset him, "at least until he's a little better adjusted." I silently agreed.

"Where's Joe?" my husband asked. "He hasn't called." No longer sure I was doing the right thing by remaining silent, I told him and prepared myself for an outburst of pain and anger.

"Is that what you've been so nervous about?" he asked. "I kept wondering if I'd done something to hurt your feelings." Then he said, "Too bad about Joe. Maybe if Joe saw my doctor he could do some good for himself."

Six months ago my husband fell apart over the smallest things, and now he handles bad news better than anyone else in our family. I know why: *he got help.* He is coping with life.

God, remind me that once sick doesn't mean he'll always be sick. Thank you that he is better. Amen.

THE REAL INSIDER

When she came home from the hospital, I said, "Please talk to me. I want to understand you."

Although my daughter is twenty-two, I don't recall that she ever talked about what was going on inside. She assumed no one cared, or, if they did, they could not understand.

"I'm different," she said. "I've always felt different from other people."

As we continued to talk, she spoke of feelings that stemmed all the way back to the time she was five years old. She felt intensely sad when her first hamster died. In trying to comfort her, I had said it was "only a hamster" and we'd buy her a new one. "He was my friend and I cried all night for him." I had no idea that she felt so strongly.

I'm now learning about my child. I'm trying to bridge twenty years of emotional silence so that I can know my real daughter.

Self-revealing God, grant me wisdom to know my real daughter—who she is inside— so I can be more loving and supportive. Amen.

DIFFERENT CHANNELS

I held his hand as we watched an old movie on TV, *The Subject Was Roses*. In the film, a son comes home from war and breakfasts with his parents. All three talk, but none of them listens. He picked this up immediately. "They're all listening to different channels," he said.

While part of my mind watched the rest of the film, another part of me pondered his acute observation. He had aptly stated our own situation. While I love him, and I do the best I can for him, we have often spoken on different channels. It was as if he couldn't listen to mine and I wouldn't listen to his.

We are making progress. I'm learning to hear what he's saying. I'm trying to think of how he feels and sees the world instead of insisting he conform to my values.

God of creation, you made us all and gave us the ability to choose our channels. Help me to tune in so that I can hear his channel without losing mine. Amen.

VALID AND INVALID

When the hospital released her from treatment, we all wanted to help. People kept volunteering to do things.

We actually did too much. We treated her almost like an invalid, not allowing her to get excited or to exert herself.

"Wait a minute," her brother said. "Are we really helping? Or are we doing so much we're making her adjustment harder?"

We talked about it, and eventually we all admitted that, from differing motives, we had done too much.

"Have we actually made her in-valid?" her brother asked. "If we don't watch ourselves, she'll certainly become an invalid. By our treatment, we have invalidated her. Let's do less, love more, and grant her validity!"

God, she is valid, and I thank you that we have stopped doing so much and are learning to treat her as a whole person. Amen.

HOPELESS

I assumed he would snap out of it or that the doctors would discover the answer to set him free. The whole family went through countless disappointments. I'd say to myself, He won't get better; it's the same old thing over and over and over.

About that time I started taking ballroom-dancing lessons through a local college. After four sessions I was ready to quit because I could not keep time with the music. I told Rosa, the best student in the class, "I'm not coming back. I'm hopeless."

"Nobody is hopeless," she said. "for some it takes longer. Don't give up. Please."

I didn't give up. I learned to keep time. But more than that, her advice opened up a new perspective on life—and especially in thinking of his illness. "Nobody is hopeless," I repeated. "For some it takes a little longer."

Thank you, God, that he isn't totally hopeless. Help me so that I won't give up hope for him. Amen.

A SPLIT FAMILY

My wife left with the final words, "I can't take any more." I wish I had understood sooner and gotten more involved. She had stayed home with our daughter; I escaped to my job.

I don't have that option now. I'm what they call the primary caregiver. I had no idea of the continuous strain—emotionally, physically, and financially. Some days I'm ready to quit. I fall asleep at night, hoping I won't have to wake up in the morning.

I wrestle with guilt for not doing more. I still hold some anger toward her mother for running out, even though I understand. I won't run away, but I'd like to. I'm here, but it's not always easy.

One thing keeps me going: my daughter needs me and I love her. Right now she has no one else because we're a split family.

God, I pray that you will unite the three of us again. But even more I pray that you'll help me be more caring for my daughter and that, as the Great Physician, you will heal her mind. Amen.

A DIFFERENT HUSBAND

I don't like all the changes he's made in the past year. "Just give me back the husband I had—the way he was before he got sick," I yelled at the doctor. "I don't know what he thinks or how he feels about anything. I knew the other man; this one is a stranger."

The doctor said, "Maybe you never did know him. You knew the way he behaved but never the real person inside."

I cried that night. And many other nights. I didn't want this supposedly improved husband. I wanted the quiet, agreeable man I had married. Now he gets angry. He wants different food. He says he hates TV. He has made a new circle of friends and I don't like most of them.

I can't go back to the husband I thought I had before. "I want to love you—the new you—as deeply as I loved the old you," I said. And I meant my words.

God, I still don't want a different husband but, despite what I want, help me to accept the new man—and to do it joyfully. Amen.

FIRMLY SPEAKING

"You don't want to talk about him because you know I'm right," she said. "He's against me. He wants me to quit so he can get somebody else." Immediately she launched into a long list of things her supervisor had done over the past five years.

I tried to change the subject, but she would come right back to it. "You don't want to talk about it because you know I'm right."

In desperation I sought professional help—for me. "I can't say to her, 'Shut up.'"

"No," the doctor agreed. "But you don't have to let her talk that way. You can say that her supervisor is one topic you don't want to talk about any more."

I had trouble cutting her off when she started on her suspicions. It was almost as if she had become addicted to her depressive mood and couldn't change. However, firm persistence paid off, and she has stopped voicing her suspicions.

God, help me to be firmly persistent and to know when and how to cut off the conversation lovingly. Amen.

FRANKLY SPEAKING

Frank, our new neighbor, appeared friendly and kind. Yet I often didn't understand what he was saying. He used common words but the sentences didn't make sense. One day his wife told of his mental illness.

Later, when my brother got sick, he developed a strange way of using common words but I couldn't figure out what he meant. I told him about Frank and said, "Whenever I don't understand, I'm going to remind you of Frank." I wanted him to know that when he spoke nonsense, I would not let him get away with it.

He has improved and now does less nonsense talking. Whenever he does revert to his nonsense, I say, "Frankly speaking . . ." and we usually both laugh. Then we talk quietly until he can explain what he means. As easy as this sounds, I have trouble confronting him, but my brother is worth the effort.

God, I'm learning to understand my brother. And understanding is a form of loving, isn't it? Amen.

BEING THERE

"Whenever you need to talk, I'm your friend," I promised my daughter. "I'll always be there for you."

A few times she's gone into a rage over simple things I've said. I've listened, but it hasn't been easy. Other times she talks about wanting to die and I have to restrain myself from pleading, "Don't talk like that."

"The most important thing," the therapist reminded me, "is not to run away emotionally. Be actively present no matter what she says."

Last week I was almost at the end of myself after her screaming obscenities and accusations. Then she paused, smiled, and said, "You know, I can talk to you now. I never could before. Now I know you care."

I left the room, glowing inside. I had been available when she needed me. Her recognition makes it easier for me to continue being there.

All-loving God, you never leave me, and that helps me in caring for her. Thank you. Amen.

A DELICATE BALANCE

I used to know how to act toward him. Then he got sick, and that upset our whole relationship.

"I don't know what to do," I said to my support group. "If I talk, I say the wrong thing. If I don't speak, he says I'm angry and need to open up."

"He's getting help," one member said. "In getting help, he inevitably changes. Previously you delicately balanced each other, but he disharmonized everything. As he gets well, you have to face the reality that your marriage can't work the same way any more."

"Are you talking about divorce?" I asked.

"I'm talking about both of you. He is already different. You have to adapt, too, for your relationship to survive."

I've been trying to find a new balance in our relationship. It's not easy because he changed. But then, I remind myself, so have I.

God, help both of us to find a new balance—a healthy one. Amen.

A PARENTHESIS

Before she got out of the hospital, I worried about how things would be. Our first ten years of marriage were great. Then she slowly slipped into depressive moods that became more severe. We were practically in divorce court before she agreed to get help.

She's better—better than she's been in a long time. She's also scared.

"I treated you so badly," she said. "I don't want to live like that again."

I explained how I had come to view our life together. "I compared your two years of illness to a parenthesis in a sentence. When we remove parenthetical expressions, the sentence still makes sense. Let's think about your illness that way—and remove the parenthesis."

God, we were so unhappy for so long—but I don't want to remember that. I want to remember the years before she got sick, and I want to concentrate on the years since—beginning with now. Amen.

THE MEMORY JAR

Two days before he came home, I made him a memory jar. On small pieces of colored paper I wrote short descriptions of the special times we had shared. I folded the slips of paper and put them inside a clear-glass cookie jar.

I wrote things like "Do you remember when we were so broke we lived for two weeks on nothing but macaroni and cheese? I loved you then. I love you now."

I handed him the memory jar nicely wrapped and said, "Whenever you have a bad day, this is my prescription for you."

He keeps the memory jar by his bed. And he does have bad times. That's when he pulls out a slip of paper and reads it. I can't provide a cure, but the memory jar is one of the things I can do to keep assuring him of my love and presence.

God, I often pause and reflect on how you've been with me through so many of the hard places. Make his memories as helpful to him as mine have been to me. Amen.

REMEMBERING

I determined to put the past behind me, but I constantly remembered her mercurial moods. Unconsciously, I expected her to repeat the old patterns of behavior. When she occasionally reverted, I'd think, You haven't changed. You're still the same.

Yet she had changed. I seldom saw the difference because I concentrated on remembering the past; she focused on the present.

Because I had trouble forgetting what went on during her worst days before she got help, I ignored the healthier woman of today. Quite slowly I recognized the change in her. I could finally say, "For a long time I remembered too much; now I want to forget the past. You're different. You've grown, and I'm beginning to like the changes."

God, at times she has a far healthier attitude than I do. As she continues to grow as a person, help me live better by forgetting the problems of the past. I always want to be thankful for the present. Amen.

FIVE

FINAL FOCUS

RELAPSE

I didn't want to consider that he might relapse.

"It's always possible," said the leader of our support group. "Nobody wants it to happen, but it does."

She pointed out signs to watch for in any kind of mental illness:

- Return of the original symptoms
- Staying in bed for long periods
- Lack of response to people
- Strange behavior, such as barricading oneself in a room
- Threatening violence
- Talking nonsense

I've learned from these friends that when relapses occur, I don't have to be devastated. They also assured me that a relapse doesn't mean a complete undoing of all the good. One of them said, "Treat him like a recovering alcoholic who falls off the wagon. He wants to get back on the wagon, so help him."

God, I ask you not to allow him to relapse. But if he does, give me wisdom and strength to handle the situation. Amen.

FROM THE BOTTOM

"She's been sick," I warned friends before they visited, "so be careful what you say."

They did exactly as I asked. Their nervousness showed; they made her uncomfortable. Her closest friend acted like the others until my wife asked, "Is something wrong?" When she said no, my wife pushed for an answer.

The friend finally told my wife about her own daughter's drug problem. My wife said, "I'm sorry." She suggested that her friend contact Narcotics Anonymous because "they can give you help or send you to the right source."

I commented to my wife about how well she handled the bad news. She said, "When you've been to the bottom the way I have, upward is the only direction to go. I learned I can handle anything if I want to." She took my hand. "And if I have support from you."

God, I'm one of those people of little faith. Thank you for what you've done for her. Now help me catch up. Amen.

LONG RECOVERY

Despite the doctor's saying, "He can go home," I insisted that he stay longer. I believed that if he stayed long enough in the hospital he would get completely well. When he came home the other two times he had improved and then lapsed into depression and erratic behavior.

"Staying longer won't cure him," she said. "It may make him worse. It's too easy for him now because he faces no challenges and has no responsibilities."

I had trouble accepting that. But after I brought him home he said, "I wanted to stay and never come home because it's safe there and I didn't have to think or do anything except take my medicine."

The doctor knew; so did my husband. I was the slow learner.

Wise God, remind me that when life gets too easy, we may be preparing for greater hardship. Push us back into action again. Amen.

FEARFUL FEELINGS

When my daughter first mentioned suicide, I said, "Miserable as life is, it beats the alternative."

Her words scared me but I did nothing, because I didn't want to think about her death. Then she tried to kill herself. During her hospitalization I visited for long periods every day, even though her talk about suicide upset me.

The caseworker said, "Be thankful she talks to you about her feelings. That's healthier than holding them inside."

"But I don't want to hear all that."

"Are you afraid? Haven't you ever had feelings like that?"

As a teenager I *had* experienced similar feelings. My daughter was reminding me of what I considered unacceptable. I didn't want to listen because she stirred up fears and memories of my own suicidal thoughts.

God of courage, help me accept my fearful feelings. Don't let me shut her off when she expresses emotions that bother me. Amen.

THE PROMISE

Our son has his own apartment and a job as part of his independent living therapy. We're allowed to visit and talk to him as much as we like.

One weekend he seemed emotionally low—the worst I had observed since his treatment.

"What's the use?" he asked. "I'm always going to be like this."

Despite our assurances he said, "Maybe I'd better end it all."

Hearing those words brought terror to my heart. I couldn't guard him every minute, so I said, "Make me one promise. If you decide to take your life, call me before you do. Promise?"

After a lengthy discussion he promised. Recently, months afterward, he said, "My dumb promise is what kept me from killing myself that weekend."

Friends in my support group have extracted similar promises from their family members, too, in such crises. And it works.

God, I've promised to love and help him. Your never-failing promises of help comfort me. Amen.

BREAKING SILENCE

I heard her veiled hints; I chose to ignore them. I remained silent because I was so certain she was better and wouldn't consider anything harmful to herself or to others. I was wrong.

She had become enraged over losing her job. She said things about her manager, such as "Her day to lose *her* job will come soon enough" or "She'll find out what she's put me through."

A few days later, my wife went back to her company. Had another employee not intervened, my wife would have stabbed her manager with a pair of scissors.

After my wife received treatment I said, "I heard your threats, and I didn't speak up or try to do anything." I promised her that I would listen—really listen—and be there to help or to call for professional intervention. "I won't let you down again."

God, I've broken the silence and I'll intervene when necessary. Make me more aware of her needs and inner pain. Amen.

THE 15 PERCENT?

Families of mental patients heard a lecture on suicide. The expert said that 85 percent of those who talk about suicide do not go through with it. She said their threats are usually a cry for help.

As I listened, I kept wondering, Who belongs in the 15 percent that actually die? How can we tell? Even if only 1 percent kill themselves, that still represents human life being destroyed.

I worried about our son. When he talked about dying, I panicked. For weeks I went through extreme tortures, wondering if he would end up in that unfavorable percentage.

After the lecture, I decided that since I have no way of knowing what he will do, I will follow what the expert said: Take threats seriously but don't panic.

God, I get scared when he talks about wanting to die. Help me to hear the real message of need. And please don't let him become part of the 15 percent. Amen.

UNTIL

Our daughter said, "The world will be a better place without me."

I debated whether my wife and I ought to try to talk her out of any suicide attempt, but we knew she would resent our efforts.

Finally, my wife said, "Problems often look worse at night. If we put off hard decisions until morning, life looks different in the sunshine." She kissed our daughter and said, "Promise me you won't make any drastic decision until morning."

A lengthy discussion followed, but she did promise. When we left, she said, "Until morning," and closed the door.

We spent a troubled night, but she phoned us the next morning. "I'm going back to the hospital," she said. "I didn't sleep. Only one word kept me from hurting myself." It was the word *until.* "It gave me something to live for—if only for a few hours. Now I know I want to keep on living."

God, thank you for until *because it offers us hope and peace. Amen.*

CALL THE EXPERT

When my husband talked about taking his life, he scared me and I didn't know what to do. At first I tried to joke with him and get his mind off the topic. It didn't work.

Then I called his doctor. I apologized for phoning, but the doctor said, "This is the time you need to call."

I accompanied my husband to the doctor's office the next day. After checking him over they increased his antidepressant medication.

"If he talks about suicide again—or even hints of it—you are to call me, night or day," the doctor said to me privately.

The doctor doesn't know how much she comforted me. Now I know that if the situation arises again, I have assistance readily available.

God, you are always ready to aid us, and usually through people. I forget so easily. Forgive me. Amen.

LETHAL WEAPONS

We've never had guns in our house, so when I heard members of my support group talk about keeping lethal weapons away from the patients, I paid little attention.

Then one evening she jabbed herself in the stomach twice with scissors before I could stop her. Fortunately, she made only superficial wounds. But from then on, I seriously considered every possible lethal weapon in the house.

She had disposable razors, and I discovered a letter opener and four sharp knives. All lethal.

To hide things only meant that she would play detective when I was out of her sight. I placed potential weapons in places where she would not automatically see them. Seeing could lead to using.

If she decides to take her life I may not be able to stop her, but I want to take all possible preventive measures.

God, give her such a desire for life that she'll forget about death. Help me to encourage that desire. Amen.

CODED MESSAGES

He had long since stopped talking about suicide, and we felt relieved. But one day a statement disturbed me—as if he was giving us a message in code. I detected something wrong, not in the words but in the subtle voice change. "That barking dog next door won't trouble me any more." I hoped he didn't plan to kill the dog, which often awakened us in the middle of the night.

After a few more coded statements I realized he was planning to take his own life. I contacted his therapist, who told me two things. First, he probably was giving me a coded message not only of intent but also a plea for help. Second, "He is serious so watch him carefully."

We kept him from carrying out his self-destructive plans. Now that we've passed that crisis I've come to understand him better and to listen for coded messages.

God, you understand my unclear messages. Enable me to understand his. Amen.

HOARDING

Quite accidentally I found her supply of pills. One word flashed into my mind: *suicide.* She's hoarding the pills until she has enough to take her life.

I kept watching her behavior and saw nothing to indicate she was thinking that way. Yet I had the evidence. I finally confronted her with the cache.

"I *have* been hoarding them," she said sheepishly. "I sneak one or two out of every bottle —just a few so you won't notice. I know I need this medicine to keep on getting better. I've been afraid that something might happen and the doctor would cut me off. If he did, I figured I'd still have enough to last me for months—in case."

With the doctor's cooperation, I keep an unopened bottle of pills in the house. The presence of the bottle assures her that, no matter what, she will have all the medicine she needs.

God, I suppose at times we all need a little extra assurance. Give it to her now. Amen.

AFTERWARD

Next year we'll both be seventy and our son will be forty-three. According to all the statistics, he will outlive us. Then what happens?

We're deeply concerned and, as his parents, we've discussed the subject often enough. He is not able to care for himself or go into an independent living situation. He needs someone.

We have no other children. A few governmental programs now provide for people like him. But we still worry. We're actively involved in setting up community services, but people are slow to respond, especially when we propose tax increases. They give research grants for cancer and AIDS—and they should—but when it comes to mental illness, we seem way down the list. And we worry.

God, as long as we're alive and able, he will have the loving care he needs. But what happens afterward? Assure us, please, that he will be cared for. Amen.

REUNION

I had not seen her for twenty-three months. I told everyone I did not want to see her again or even to think about her. She was not only mentally unbalanced, she had tried to kill me.

A chaplain at the hospital contacted me and begged me to visit. "Your presence could greatly affect her improvement."

Reluctantly I agreed to visit "for a few minutes."

When I saw her, something happened inside of me. Impulsively I embraced her and heard myself say, "I love you and I forgive you."

Until that moment I hated her and never wanted to see her again. But on seeing her again, a miracle took place—the rekindling of my love. A month after my visit, she came home for the weekend. If she continues to improve, she'll soon be well enough to live at home.

I'm surprised again, but now I want her home—with me.

God, thank you for rekindling my love. Forgive me for my neglect. Amen.

NOT SEEING HIM AGAIN

The first time we committed him, and the second time he voluntarily reentered treatment. As he got out of the car, I thought, I don't ever want to see you again. I hope they keep you locked up until you die.

Immediately a wave of guilt swept over me for having such strong emotions, but I really felt that way—at least right then. As I drove away I thought, If he died, I could get over my pain and start to live again. But he's not dead; he's not fully alive either. He is in my life just enough to keep me off balance.

By the time I got home, my thoughts had progressed until I said aloud, "I do love him." I get upset over his illness and I worry that he'll never recover. Even with all the negative thoughts that float through my head, I haven't really stopped loving him.

God, my emotions hit the entire range from high to low. Remind me that despite my feelings I am committed to him. Amen.

LIGHTING CANDLES

I had no idea what would happen to her. I had
never known anyone hospitalized before. The
staff gave me vague answers and nothing
concrete about her chances for improvement
and wouldn't discuss total recovery. I got
angry. I demanded, I accused them of incom-
petence. They still couched their words carefully. "We have a high recovery rate for
people like her" was the strongest assurance I
could get.

I left angry, silently railing against the unfair-
ness of life and the lack of answers.

I went into the chapel and a woman came in,
knelt, then lit a candle. From the recesses of
my mind, I recalled the statement, "It is
better to light one candle than to curse the
darkness."* I had been cursing darkness by
demanding answers. I decided then to light a
candle—to hold on to the words of hope the
staff had given me.

*God, I'd like total light but I'm willing to
light one candle—to hope. Amen.*

---

*Motto of the Christophers.

TOMORROW?

Today was a wonderful time. Everything went right all day. Perfect weather. Happy mood. No stress. He behaved so well no observer would ever have known of his mental illness.

Today was wonderful. I allowed myself to enjoy each experience. That's how I cope with life. I can't presume about tomorrow; I don't even want to think about tomorrow. I survive emotionally by being thankful for the present.

I used to devote so much energy toward preparing myself for the unknown. I would have said to myself, Yesterday he behaved as well as he did today. But tomorrow?

People like us, caregivers, have no guarantees about the future. We have no tomorrow—only today.

God, thank you for the comforting words, "So do not worry about tomorrow; it will have enough worries of its own. There is no need to add to the troubles each day brings."* Because you're with us. Amen.

*Matthew 6:34, TEV.

OUT OF THE CLOSET

As parents, family members, and friends, we're proud of ourselves. We love and provide care for mentally sick individuals. We're present when they need us.

In the beginning we didn't talk outside our family about the mentally ill person. But now some of us have come out of the closet. We tell other people because we have nothing to be ashamed of. Many of us have become activists for the cause of the mentally ill. We're not hiding our loved ones in sealed-off institutions. We're telling our stories and asking people to help as individuals. They can assist through political involvement and legislative pressure. We urge corporations to provide grants for further study. And we realize that not only does this activism help our loved ones, it gives us a deep sense of satisfaction.

God, I want to be able to say at the end of my life, "I did what I could." With your encouraging support, I can do that. Amen.

ADDITIONAL RESOURCES

Support Organizations

Emotions Anonymous, P.O. Box 4245, St. Paul, MN 55104.

National Alliance for the Mentally Ill, 1901 North Fort Myer Drive, Suite 500, Arlington, VA 22209.

Recovery, Inc., 116 South Michigan Avenue, Chicago, IL 60003.

Recommended Reading

Newsletters and pamphlets

NAMI Newsletter, published bimonthly by National Alliance for the Mentally Ill.

U.S. Department of Health and Human Services. National Institute of Mental Health. *Depressive Disorders: Causes and Treatment.* 1983.

U.S. Department of Health and Human Services. *Medicine for the Layman: Depression and Manic Depressive Illness.* 1982.

Books

George Bennett. *When the Mental Patient Comes Home.* Christian Care Books. Philadelphia: Westminster Press, 1980.

Agnes B. Hatfield. *Coping with Mental Illness in the Family: A Family Guide.* Arlington, Va.: NAMI, 1984.

E. Fuller Torrey. *Surviving Schizophrenia: A Family Manual.* New York: Harper & Row, 1983.